WORLD GEOGRAPHY

TIME & CLIMATE ZONES

LATITUDE, LONGITUDE, TROPICS, MERIDIAN AND MORE

**GEOGRAPHY FOR KIDS
5TH GRADE SOCIAL STUDIES**

Speedy Publishing LLC

40 E. Main St. #1156

Newark, DE 19711

www.speedypublishing.com

Copyright 2017

In this book, we're going to talk
about time and climate zones
of the world. So, let's get right to it!

The lines of latitude and longitude on a map help us with many things. They are used to pinpoint an exact location on the entire surface of the Earth. They are also used to separate time zones from each other. You can get a sense of the general climate of an area based on its location using the imaginary lines of latitude and longitude. They are like a giant imaginary grid on the Earth.

DISTRICT OF
TERRITORIES
KEEWATIN
HUDSON BAY
MANITOBA
Eskimo Point
Churchill
REINDEER LAKE
Flin Flon
Norway House
Yorkton
Brandon
Regina
N DAK
Williston
Bismarck
Fargo
MINN
Duluth
L. SUPERIOR
Sault Ste. Marie
Sudbury
ONTARIO
Ft. William
Port Arthur
Timmins
Ft. Albany
LAKE OF THE WOODS
Winnipeg
BLACK HILLS
S DAK
Pierre
Minneapolis
St. Paul
WIS
Green Bay
Superior
Madison
Milwaukee
NEBR
Omaha
Des Moines
IOWA
MISSOURI
PLATTE
Lincoln
KANS
Denver
Topeka
Wichita
Kansas City
Chicago
ILL
Springfield
IND
Indianapolis
Gary
Detroit
Toledo
Cleveland
OHIO
Columbus
Cincinnati
PA
Pittsburg
Buffalo
Rochester
Toronto
New York
ARKANSAS
OKLA
Amarillo
Tulsa
Oklahoma City
RED
Jefferson City
MO
St. Louis
Louisville
KY
Frankfort
Nashville
TENN
W VA
VA
Richmond
Washington
Baltimore
Philadelphia
DEL
C. Hatteras
GULF STREAM
TEXAS
Ft. Worth
Dallas
Waco
LA
Little Rock
Memphis
MISSISSIPPI
Birmingham
ALA
Montgomery
MISS
Jackson
Chattanooga
Atlanta
GA
Columbus
NC
Raleigh
Charlotte
SC
Columbia
Augusta
Charleston
Savannah
Shreveport
Baton Rouge
Mobile
COLO
PECOS
RIO GRANDE
Austin
Houston
San Antonio
Corpus Christi
Brownsville
Matamoros
Monterrey
Ciudad Victoria
Tampico
San Luis Potosi
Querétaro
Mexico City
GULF OF CAMPECHE
Mérida
YUCATÁN
Cabo Catoche
YUCATÁN CHANNEL
Havana
Cienfuegos
I. of Pines
New Orleans
Tallahassee
FLA
Tampa
St. Petersburg
Jacksonville
C. Kennedy
Ft. Lauderdale
Miami
EVERGLADES
Bahama Is (Br)
Great Abaco I
Andros I
Nassau
Cat I
GULF OF MEXICO
MEXICAN BASIN
STRAITS OF FLORIDA
NORTH AMERICAN BASIN
WEST INDIES
ANTILLES
CURRENT
ATLANTIC
NORTH AMERICA
UNITED STATES
CANADA

WHY ARE THERE TIME ZONES?

The Earth turns and makes a complete rotation in 24 hours. This is why an Earth day consists of 24 hours of time. Other planets spin too, but their days or the time it takes for them to make a complete rotation, are not the same amount of time as Earth's days are.

When we visualize the Earth turning, we imagine that it is turning on a pole called an axis, but, of course, there isn't a pole really there. It's just an imaginary device to help us understand how the Earth rotates.

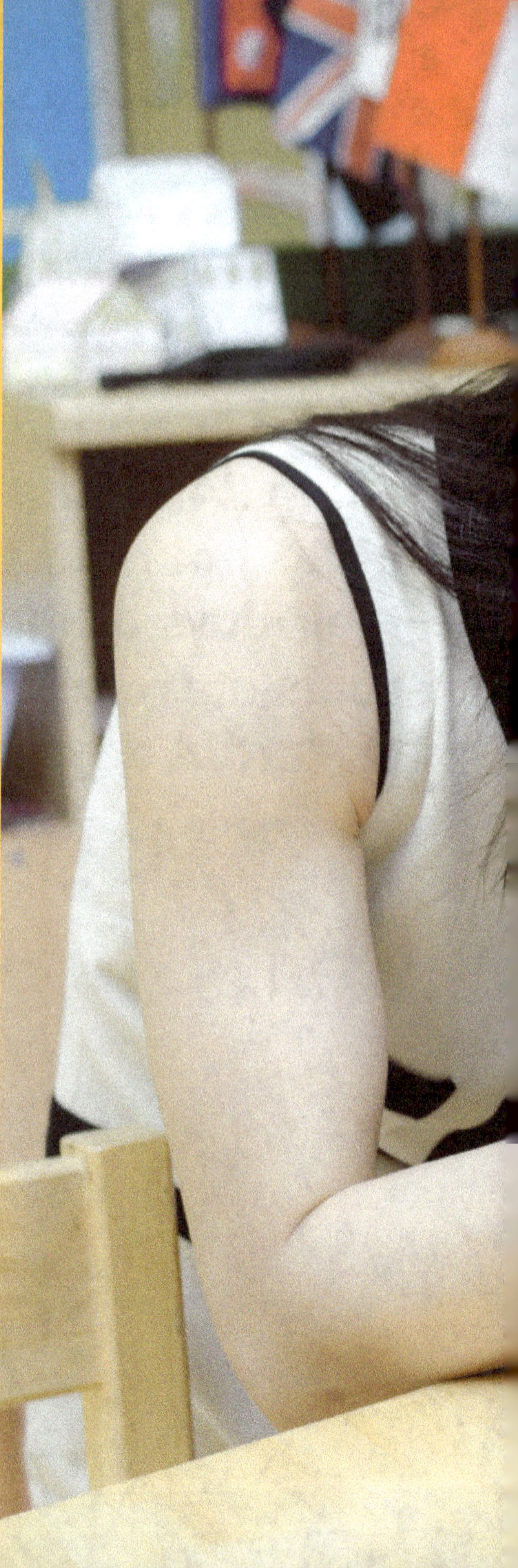

It might be morning where you are located right now, but on the opposite side of the Earth, it's the middle of the night. As the Earth turns, different locations are either receiving sunlight during the day or not receiving any sunlight at night.

f there were only one time zone for all of Earth, noon would represent different things to different locations. It might be midday for some locations, but it might be morning, evening or nighttime for others.

The Earth's Rotation

oward the end of the 1800s when transportation was starting to get a lot faster, scientists got together to figure out a way to have different zones of time around the world. They researched the way the Earth moved on its axis to come up with a system that could be used everywhere.

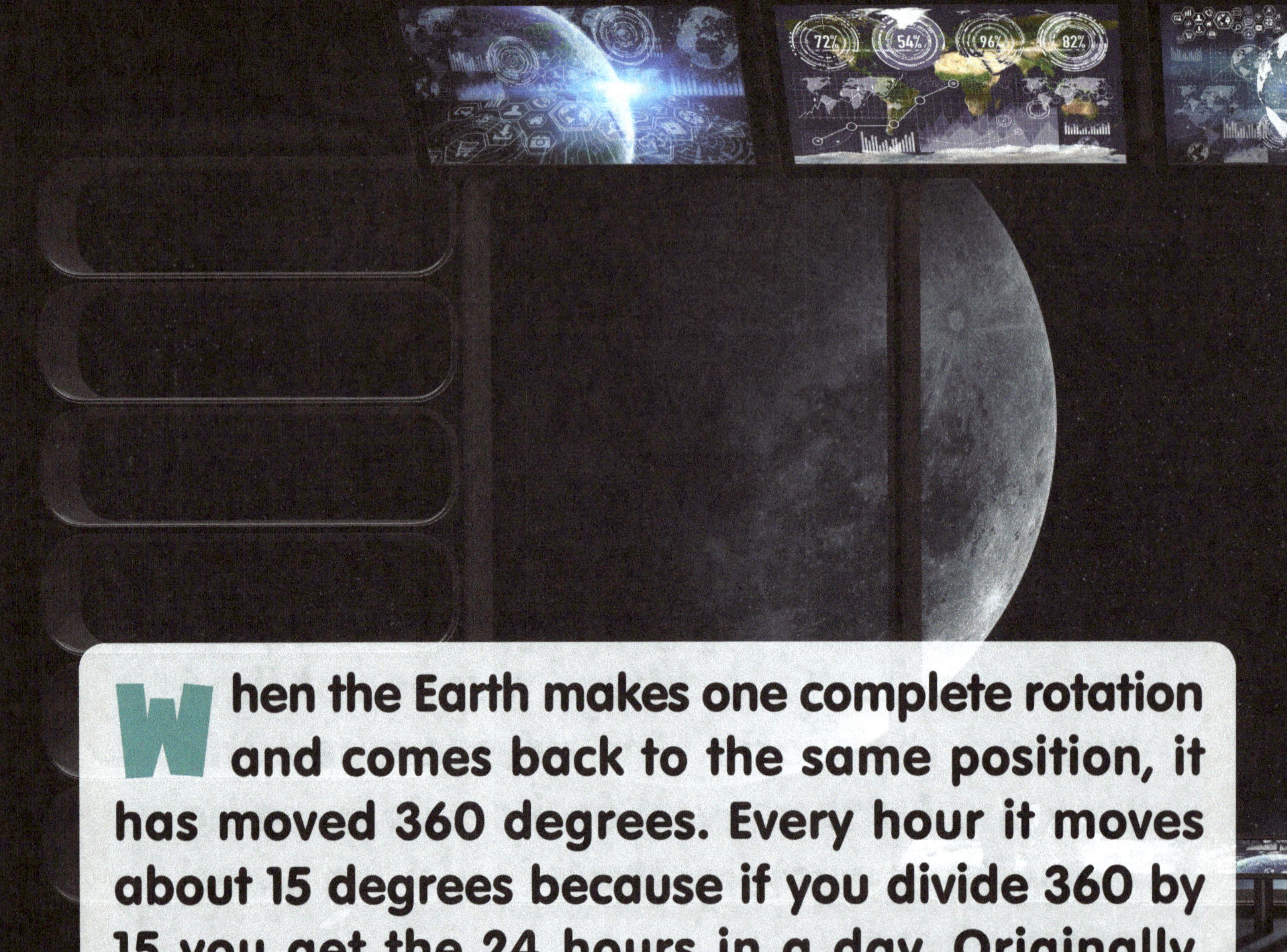

When the Earth makes one complete rotation and comes back to the same position, it has moved 360 degrees. Every hour it moves about 15 degrees because if you divide 360 by 15 you get the 24 hours in a day. Originally, scientists divided up the Earth into 24 sections, which created 24 different time zones. Within a specific time zone, the same standard time is used.

ASTRONAUTS STUDYING THE PLANET EARTH

LONGITUDE

WHAT IS LONGITUDE?

Imagine that you have a globe. The North Pole is at the top of the globe and the South Pole is at the bottom. If you start at the top at the North Pole and then draw a line to the South Pole you would have a longitude line, which is also called a meridian. The line is curved and bulges out at the equator.

These imaginary lines would need to be drawn 1 degree apart from each other, so there would be 360 longitude lines to travel the 360 degrees around the sphere.

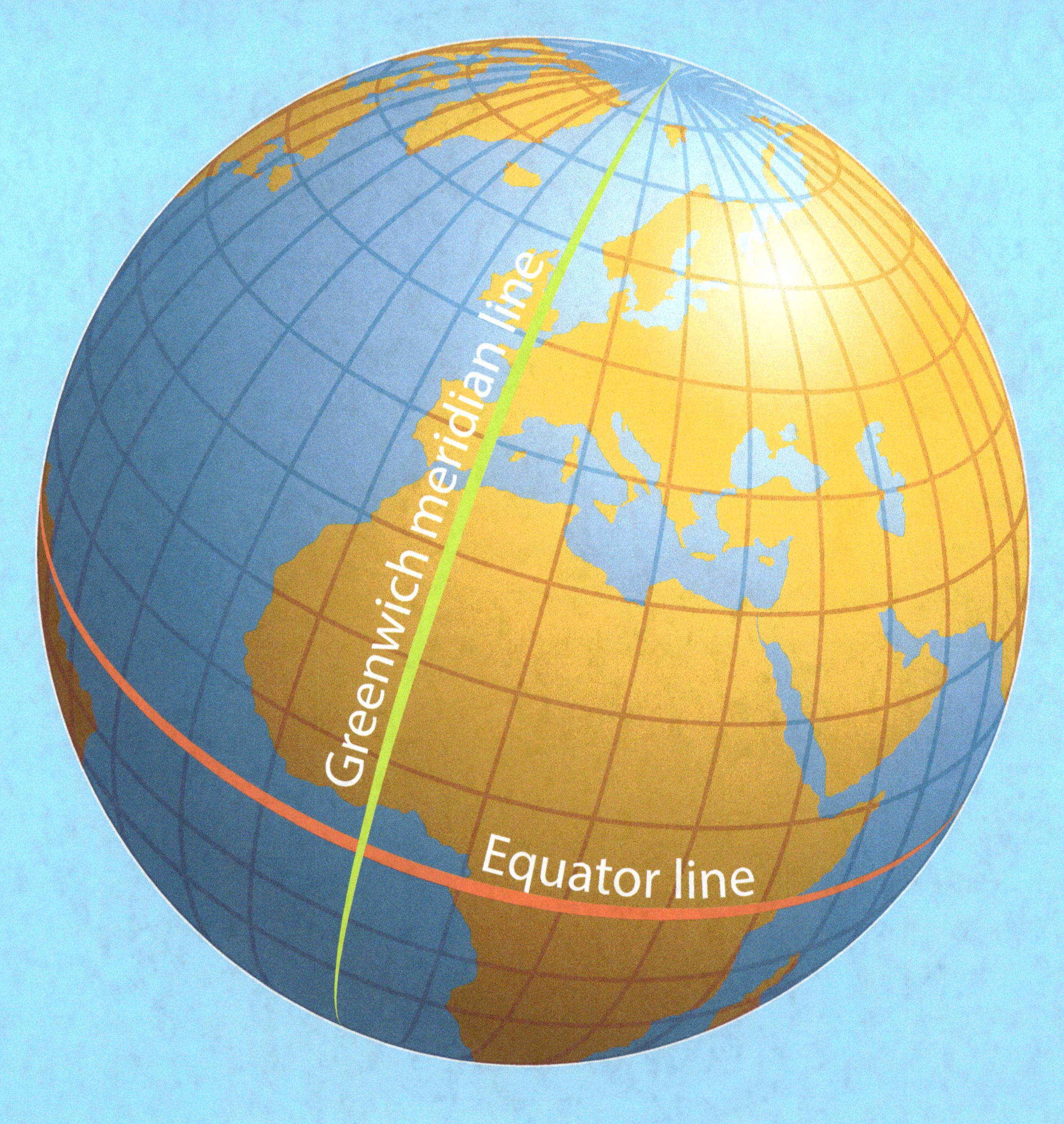

Greenwich meridian line
Equator line

At the equator, since it is going from east to west, the longitude lines would make a right angle with the equator. There would be 15 degrees or 15 longitude lines for every time zone. You'll notice that the lines are closer to each other at the north pole or south pole and they are the maximum distance apart at the equator, about 69 miles apart. When you divide the length of the equator 24,874 miles by 360 this is approximately what you get--69 miles. The meridians converge to a common point both at the North Pole and at the South Pole.

The equator separates the world into a Northern Hemisphere to the north and a Southern Hemisphere to the south. However, to separate the world to describe it as an Eastern Hemisphere and a Western Hemisphere, the scientists had to pick a location. They picked the royal observatory for astronomers at Greenwich, England.

ROYAL OBSERVATORY, GREENWICH PARK, LONDON ENGLAND

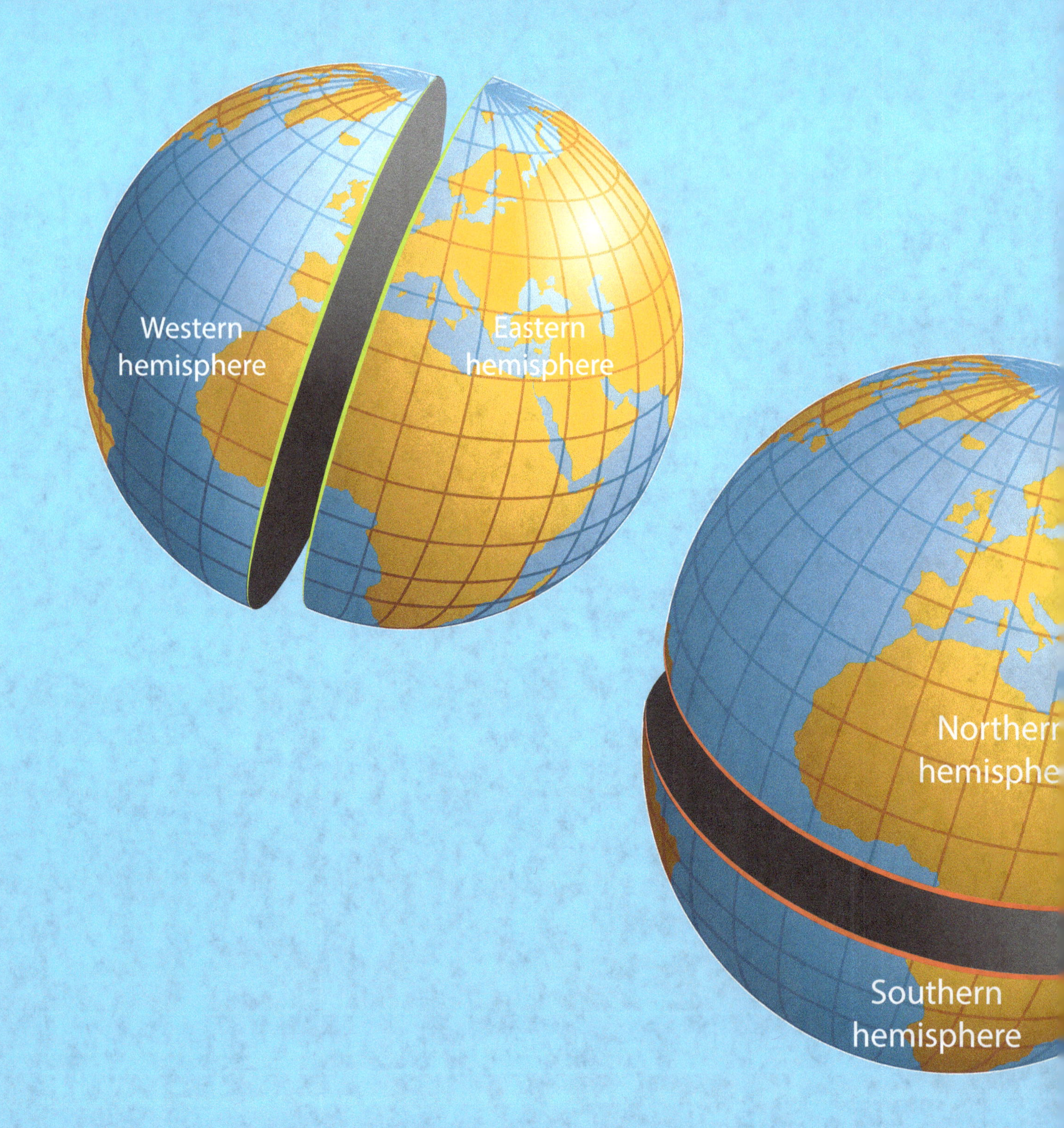

Western
hemisphere
Eastern
hemisphere
Northern
hemisphere
Southern
hemisphere

The meridian or line of longitude that goes through Greenwich is called the Prime Meridian and is the longitude of 0 degrees. Everything that lies in a position that is east of the Prime Meridian until you reach the meridian located on the opposite side of the Earth is the Eastern Hemisphere. Everything that lies west of the Prime Meridian until you reach the meridian located on the opposite side of the Earth is the Western Hemisphere.

Of course, there are locations in between different degrees of longitude as well. One degree is equivalent to 60 minutes and one minute is equivalent to 60 seconds so you can use these to give more precise measurements.

1 min

GREENWICH WATCH
GALVANO MAGNETIC CLOCK

TIME ZONES AND LONGITUDE

The time at the Prime Meridian at Greenwich is described as Greenwich Mean Time or GMT. When you travel west toward the United States every section measuring 15 degrees represents a time zone, which is an hour earlier than the time in Greenwich. Every time zone east of Greenwich is one hour later than the time in Greenwich.

This means that it doesn't make any difference where you are; if it is noontime the sun is the highest in the sky and midnight divides the night in half from sunset to sunrise.

For example, if you reside in New York City, New York, during standard time your time zone is GMT – 5, which is five time zones in a western direction from Greenwich.

CANADA
UNITED STATES
MEXICO
ATLANTIC OCEAN
PACIFIC OCEAN
VENEZUELA
COLOMBIA
ECUADOR
PERU
BRAZIL
BRASILIA
BOLIVIA
LA PAZ
CHILE
ARGENTINA
N
E
S
W

New-York

ATLANTIC
IRELAND
PORTUGAL
SPAIN
FRANCE
ITALY
MOROCCO
ALGERIA
LIBYA
EGY
MALI
NIGER
CHAD
SUDA
IVORY COAST
ZAIRE
ANGOLA

Lon

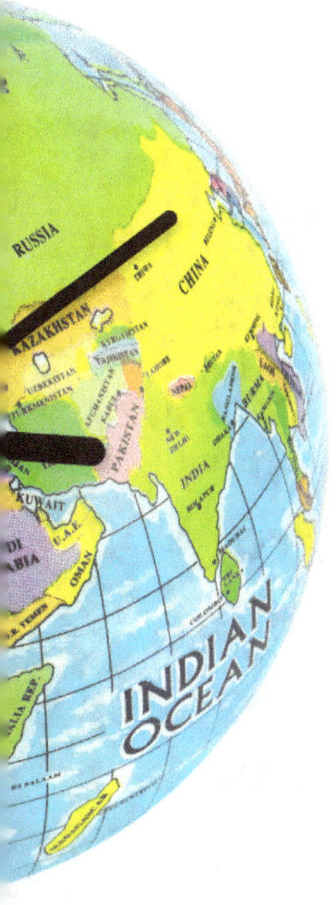

So this means that if it's 8 pm in New York on December 1, when it's standard time in New York, then it would be 1 am in Greenwich, the following day, because you are 5 time zones or 5 hours earlier. Daylight Savings Time changes these time periods.

In the United States, there are four time zones: Eastern, Central, Mountain, and Pacific. During Standard Time, if it's 4 pm on the West Coast it would be 5 pm in the Mountain time zone, 6 pm in the Central time zone, and 7 pm in the Eastern time zone.

Longitude determines time zones, but both longitude and latitude are needed to determine locations.

TIME ZONES WORLD MAP

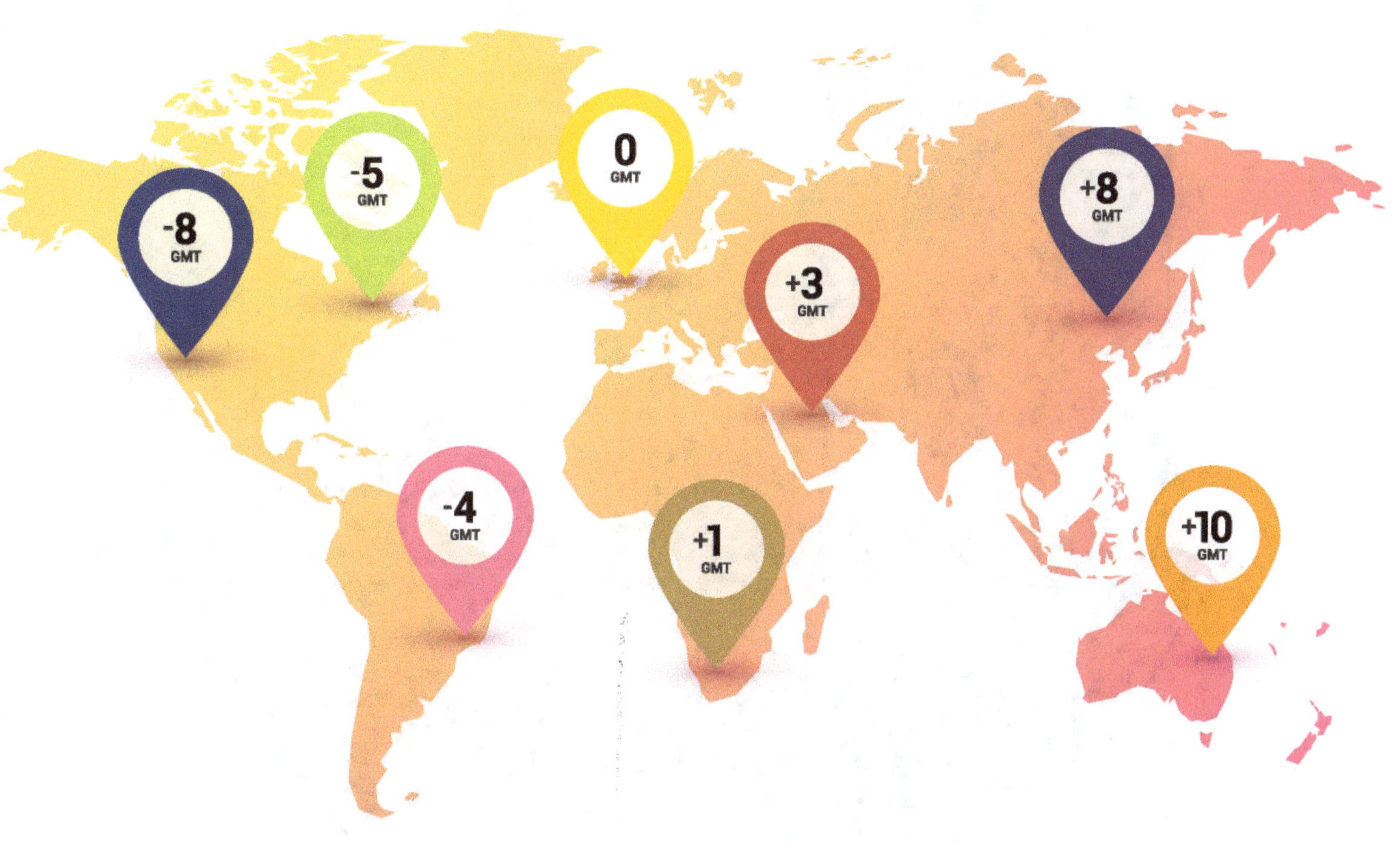

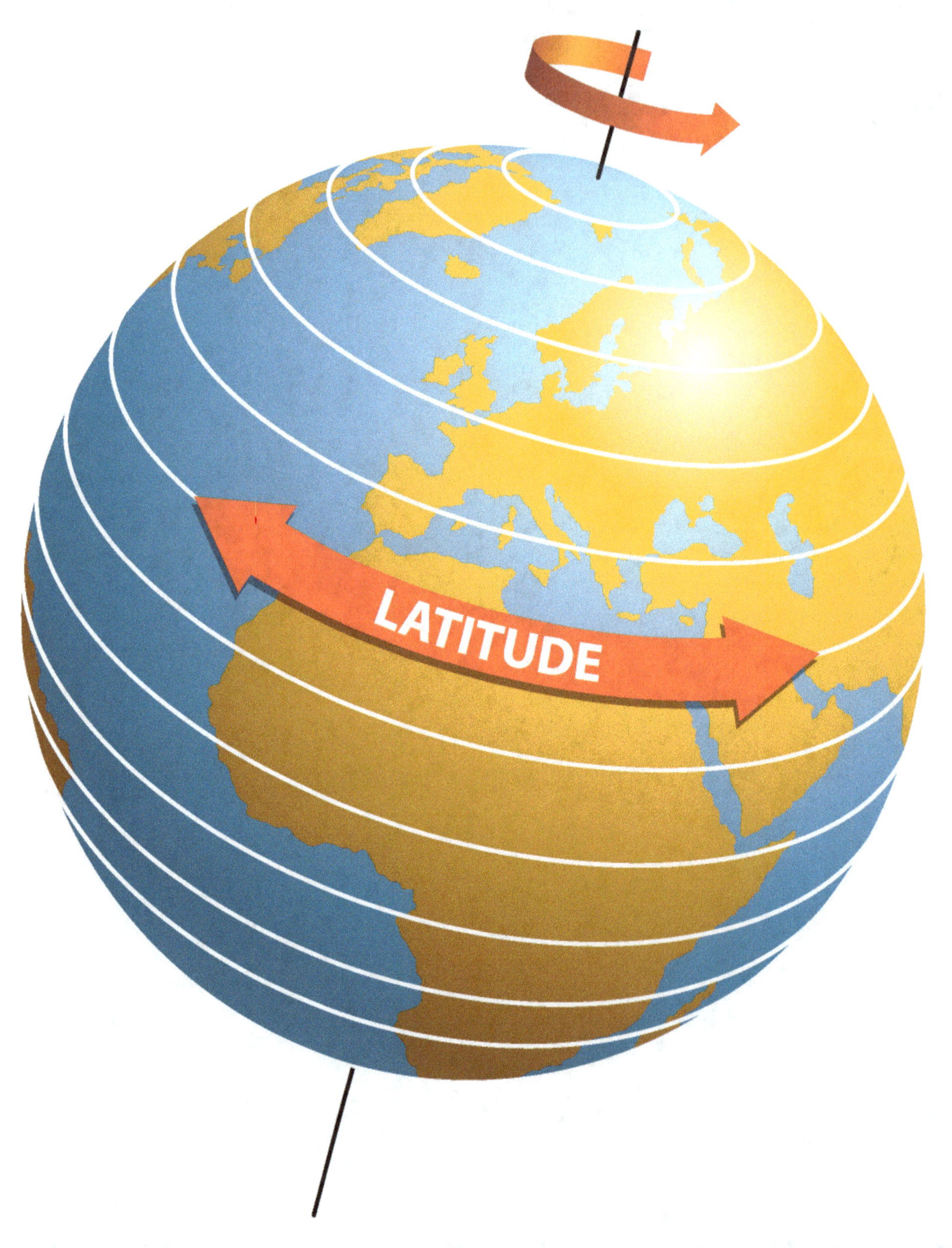

LATITUDE

WHAT IS LATITUDE?

Just as longitude lines provide the east-west position of a location, latitude lines provide a location's north-south position. Lines of latitude are like hoops around the Earth from east to west. Unlike lines of longitude, they don't converge at any points but are always the same distance from each other.

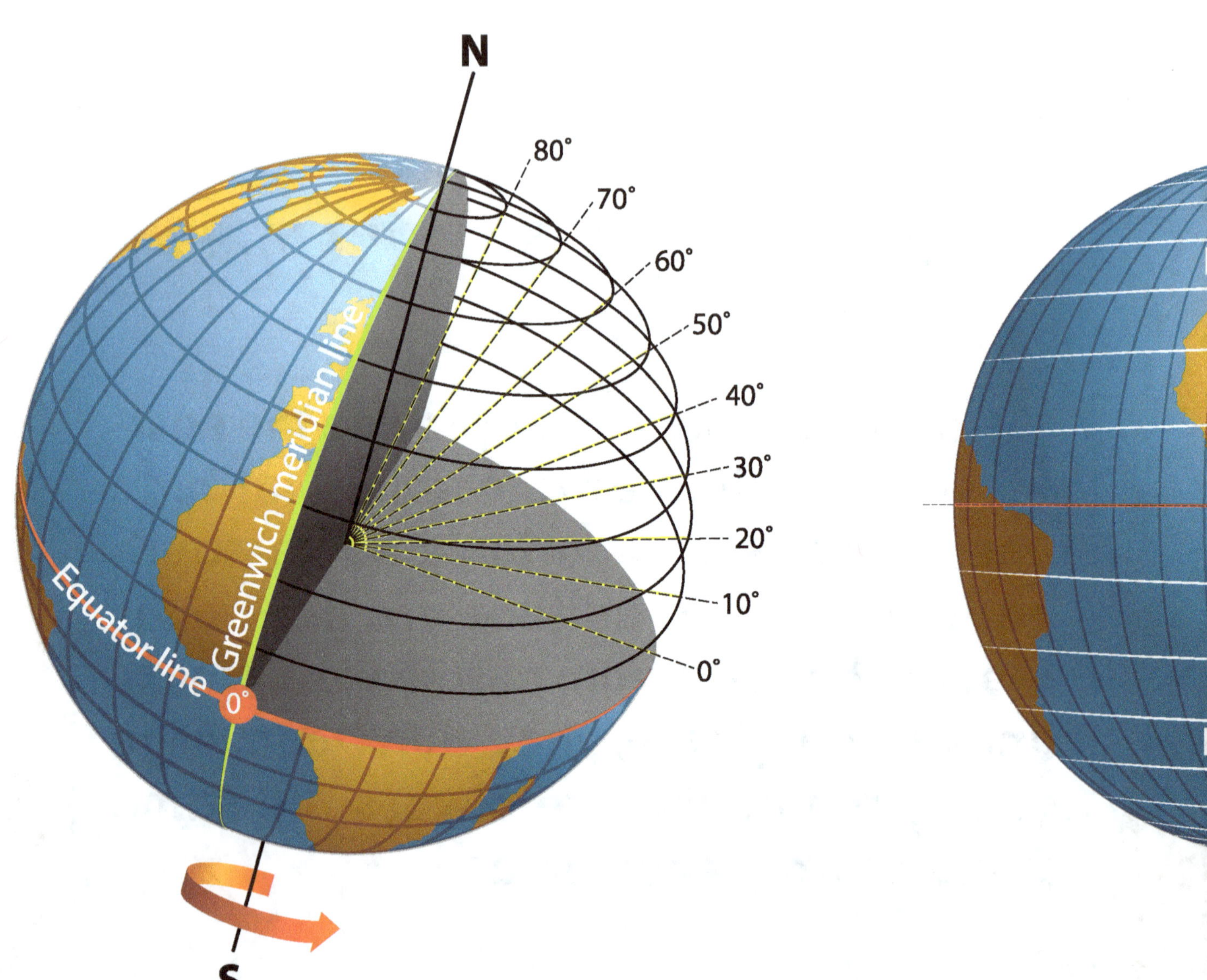

N
80°
70°
60°
50°
40°
30°
20°
10°
0°
Greenwich meridian line
Equator line
0°
S

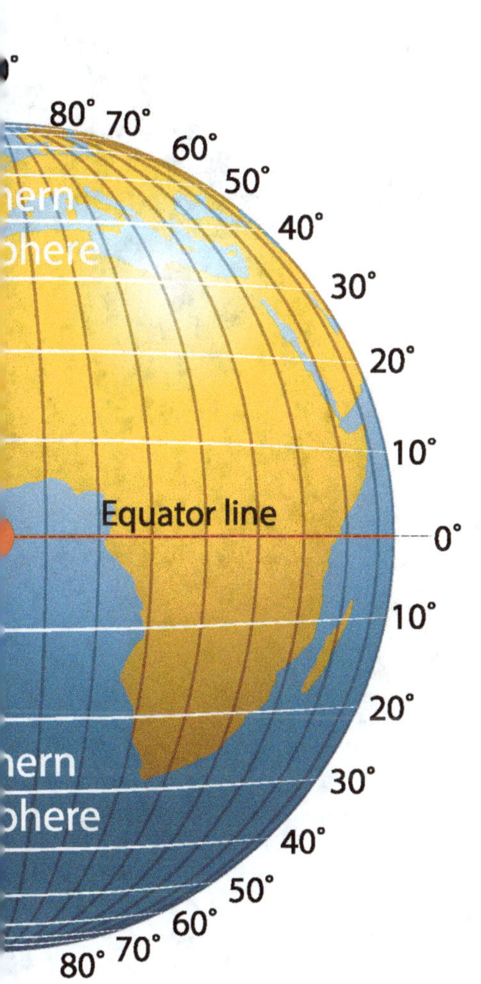

They are about 69 miles from each other. The equator is at 0 degrees. Latitude lines above the equator are designated with north and lines below the equator are designated with south. On a flat map, latitude lines are horizontal while longitude lines are vertical. There are 180 lines or degrees of latitude.

Here are some important latitudes from north to south.

- The Arctic Circle, 66.5 degrees north
- The Tropic of Cancer, 23.5 degrees north
- The Equator, 0 degrees of latitude
- The Tropic of Capricorn, 23.5 degrees south
- The Antarctic Circle, 66.5 degrees south

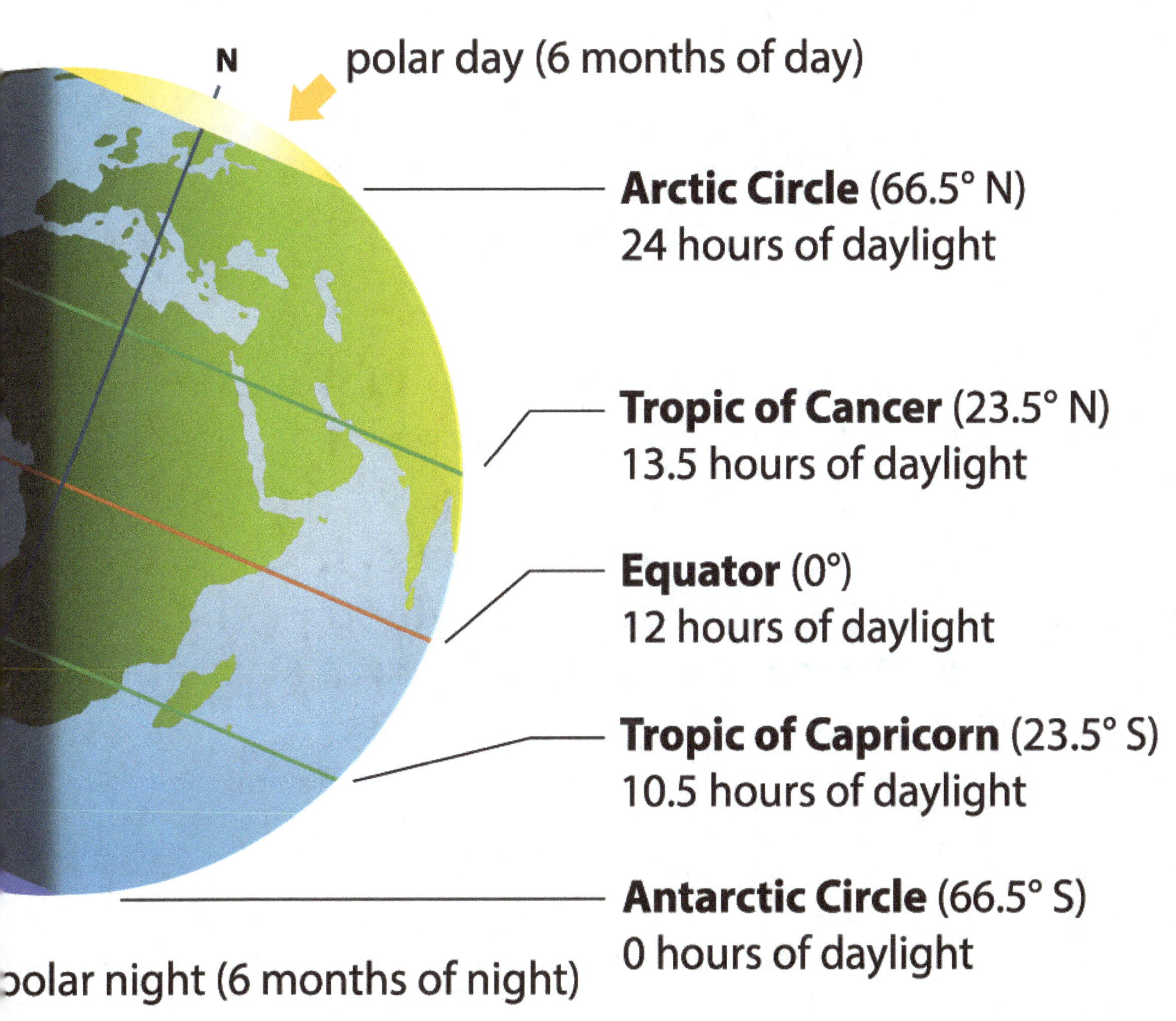

N
polar day (6 months of day)
Arctic Circle (66.5° N)
24 hours of daylight
Tropic of Cancer (23.5° N)
13.5 hours of daylight
Equator (0°)
12 hours of daylight
Tropic of Capricorn (23.5° S)
10.5 hours of daylight
Antarctic Circle (66.5° S)
0 hours of daylight
polar night (6 months of night)

WHAT ARE THE TROPICS?

The equator represents the part of the Earth where the temperature is the hottest. The landmasses in the world that lie between the Tropic of Cancer and the Tropic of Capricorn are described as the Tropics. These areas have sultry heat, heavy rainfall, and dense rainforests.

The regions that fall north of the Tropic of Cancer and south of the Tropic of Capricorn have four distinct seasons. However, when it's summer in the Northern Hemisphere, then it's winter in the Southern Hemisphere and vice versa.

LATITUDE AND LONGITUDE OF A LOCATION

There are many different ways to write the exact location of a city or other geographical location. For example, the location of New York City can be written the following ways.

COMPASS ON A WORLD MAP

ALBANY
Troy
Pittsfield
Mas
Catskill
Mountains
Slide Mtn
149
Chicop
Westfield
Torrington
HART
178
Liberty
Monticello
Newburgh
ATERBURY
127
New Milford
NEW HA
84
Middletown
Milford
Ossining
Danbury
230
209
Suffern
Norwalk
BRIDGE
206
YONKER
STAMFORD
PATERSON
New
Rochelle
Jefferson
Netcong
NEWARK JERSEY CITY
495
aston
ELIZABETH
Hempstead
Bay
Shore
Fire
TOWN
Somerville
Staten I
NEW YOR
101
Perth Amboy
Statue of Libe
Princeton
Red Bank
111
Long Branch
38
Trenton
158
Asbury Park
36
195
165
Levittown
Lakewood
New
Point Pleasant
Hudso
Independence Hall
Toms River
82
HILADELPHIA

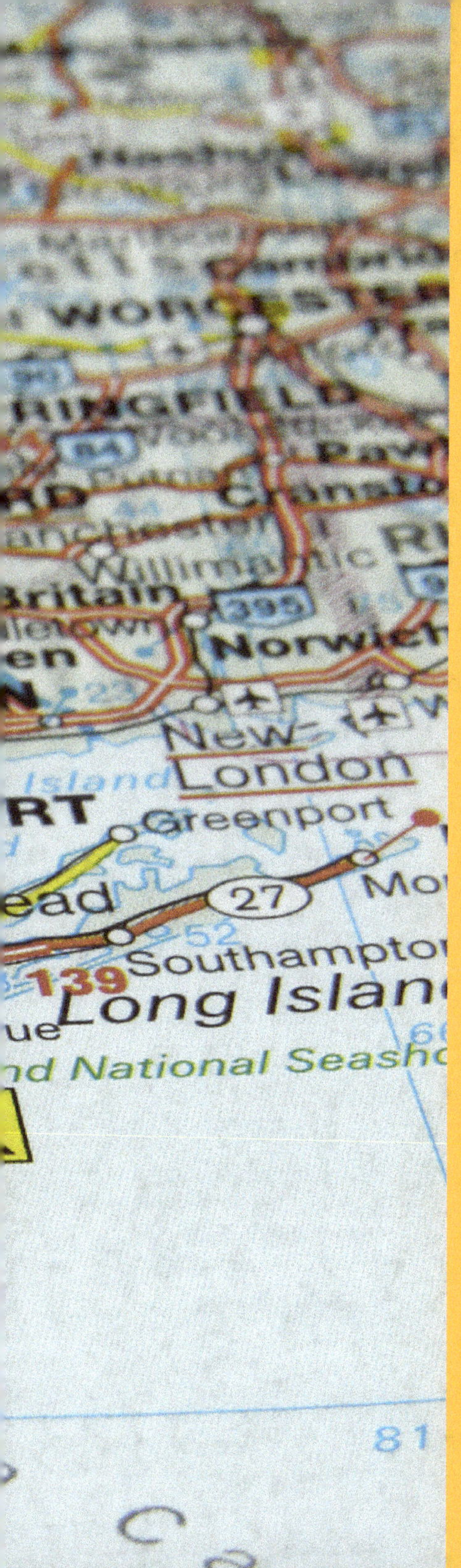

- **Geographic Coordinates of New York City, New York**

  Latitude: 40 degrees 42 minutes 51 seconds North (of the Equator)
  Longitude: 74 degrees 00 minutes 21 seconds West (of the Prime Meridian)

- **With symbols, this is written as:**

  Latitude: 40° 42' 51"
  Longitude: 74° 00' 21"

- **Coordinates in decimal degrees for New York City, New York**

  Latitude: 40.7142700°
  Longitude: -74.0059700°

- **Coordinates of New York in degrees and decimal minutes**

  Latitude: 40° 42.8562'
  Longitude: 74° 0.3582'

HALIFAX
WESTGRÖNLAND
OSTGRÖNLAND
AZOREN
MONTREAL
WASHINGTON
NEW YORK
HAVANNA
NEW ORLEANS
MEXIKO-STADT
BRASILIA
RIO DE JANEIRO
SÃO PAULO
MONTEVIDEO
BUENOS AIRES
CARACAS
LA PAZ
ASUNCIÓN
SANTIAGO de CHILE
PANAMA
SANTAFÉ de BOGOTÁ
QUITO
LIMA
GUATEMALA-
STADT

WORLD CLOCK

GMT VERSUS UTC

In 1972, the GMT was replaced by a more accurate way of measuring time, UTC, which stands for Universal Coordinated Time. Atomic clocks made it possible to measure the rotation of the Earth with more accuracy. For example, on December 31, a second of time is added or subtracted from the world's clock to synchronize GMT and UTC.

Even geological events can alter the rotation of the Earth. When Japan had a 9.0 magnitude earthquake, it shifted mass away from the equator and the Earth's day was shortened by 1.8 microseconds, which is one millionth of a second.

SUMMARY

T he lines of longitude and latitude are like an invisible grid on the Earth. The longitude lines establish the distance from the prime meridian at Greenwich, dividing the Earth into 24 different time zones. By using latitude and longitude, you can pinpoint a location anywhere on the Earth's surface. If a location on Earth lies between the Tropic of Cancer in the north and the Tropic of Capricorn in the south, then it has a tropical climate. Landmasses north of these two special latitudes have four seasons of the year, although if the Northern Hemisphere is experiencing summer, the Southern Hemisphere is experiencing winter.

Awesome! Now that you've read about the world's time and climate zones, you may want to read more about world geography in the Baby Professor book *Five Major Islands of the World – Geography Books for Kids 5-7 | Children's Geography Books.*

Visit

www.BabyProfessorBooks.com

to download Free Baby Professor eBooks
and view our catalog of new and exciting
Children's Books